Grey Wolf Speaks

Danny Roberts

Introduction
By
L. Henry Dowell

Edited By Kelsey Shea

Black Box Publishing

Table of Contents

Introduction

If you live in the Southeast, you'll find that everyone you meet claims to be at least one quarter Indian. While this may seem incredible to some, and has been the subject of numerous jokes, the truth is, it's entirely possible.

The Cherokee Indians who hunted Kentucky and the lands of the Southeastern United States were a proud and distinguished race, who lived off the land, and in many cases learned to live in peace with the white man. Intermarrying with white settlers was actually a very common practice, and many children of these unions went on to become important leaders within the tribe. It was from one of these unions the poet Grey Wolf was descended.

I have known the man called Grey Wolf for forty years now, and in that time I have seen him grow from a boy into a man. From a son to a father and then a grandfather. He is my cousin and friend. It was around his thirtieth year that he sought to reconnect with his Native American roots. Always a lover of the outdoors, it was Grey Wolf who opened my children's eyes to a way of life that's been lost to many of us, myself included. Exploring the ancient hunting grounds where we were raised, Grey Wolf introduced them to the joy of wading creeks, shooting the bow and arrow, playing reed flutes and horseback riding. Great fun for kids who have spent their lives in the suburbs. Helping to assemble his work into this book has been my way of saying thank you.

The poems and stories contained within this volume deal with Life and Death, Love, Nature and Dreams. Although contemporary, they are written from a Native American perspective. In that respect, they are best consumed around the light of a campfire surrounded by loved ones.

-L. Henry Dowell, Playwright and Publisher

Grey Wolf Speaks

Spirit of the Wolf,
Guide me with your calm stature,
Speak to me with your eyes,
Touch me with your softness,
Sing to me from your mountain,
Warm my cold heart with your warm fur.
Feed me from the land,
From your hand.
Protect me in the night.
Guide me to the light.
Gray shadows follow me.
Following two wolves,
Left and right.
We need each other,
Like the moon to the sun.
Dawn to night.
I am the Grey Wolf.
Born of the Wolf Clan.

Life and Death

1000 Years

I have thought and I have prayed,
All I can say is,
I will try to show you a great time,
No more promise I cannot keep.
Don't measure my wealth for I am only rich in nature.
Enter my door to my Spirit world, sip some wine,
Taste sweetness peach schnapps.
See ever more clear.
Wrap you in my flag the blood has sweated through.
Stop to breathe hesitate as we climb this mountain.
Head's swimming, I get so dizzy.
I bend and fold like a wintered flower, crumble ever so easy.
Watching the last breath freeze my face.
Racing horse hearts flushes my face.
Night grows cold slips away like a dream,
A memory no one can steal.
1000 years the tears fall as rain upon my feet.
I have no more answers, no more questions.
Tails dancing feet, heartbeat drums,
Laughter soft like a fallen fog.
Floating candles upon the water,
Burning desires from the night.

Life Everlasting

Searching high to low,
Growing natural rich ground.
Gathering bundles in the arm.
Autumn beauty of frost.
Opening golden eye flowers.
On the rivers in the mountains.
Sweet taste of your aroma.
Dances in the air.
Replenish life everlasting.
Only when we stop growing,
Then we grow old.
Forsaken beauty of young.
Walk lightly watching.
Eagle flies by.
Sitting in a pine tree.
Spirit talk to me.
Make us whole in this life.
Taking breath from life everlasting.
Old man in the clay pipe.
Cane stem hollow life.
Gathering forked rivers.

Gifts

To wait till tomorrow,
Why you can wait no more,
Like a child at heart,
You can take no more.
Thinking tomorrow will never come,
Like a day that never ends.
Your gift is here today.
Same as another day.
Just dream tonight,
Together we will have another day.
Smile before you shut your eyes,
Dancing in your dreams, thoughts of tomorrow.
Told you it would not be long,
Aren't you glad we had today.
Was not as bad as you thought it was,
Gifts from today are gifts from yesterday.

Winter Chills

Tired of keeping enemies as my friends.
Time goes fast, things grow old.
Don't have air any more, no longer free.
What it is like not to think.
Too weak to crawl from the floor.
Take my hand no more.
What has been, what will be.
Winter carries my bones to summer.
When you chill from the sweat.
Days so exhausted, nights even worse.
Letting life run his course.
Free from pills down the drain.
Today won the battle,
No more broken bones.
In life one has only one true friend.
There was a beginning now they are in the end.
Tell no more lies, seek me no more.
Have no more air to give, done used up.
Seen in the moon hunting coons.

Spirit of Life Breathe in Me

The moon pulls the blanket of clouds over to dream,
As we dream open the doors.
Fears within fears,
We must face once again.
Follow the bear tracks in the dusty sands of time.
Shall we be man to face the bear with a weapon,
Or shall we face the bear with only our Spirit within?
As we stand, then walk,
Then run through life as a bear,
More than man can bare.
Must we search who we are?
We, who call upon one God, one Creator
To guide us who we be,
Then how we be who we not be?
For no matter what man must believe,
Man must acknowledge in the beginning was man.
Then man became many lost upon his journey.
Feed me the plant, then I become the plant.
Feed me meat then I become the meat.
Hybrids in our own time.

Hope Floats

From Mothers womb new life shall drop.
Another cycle, giving life, never to stop.
Taking a life to a dark grave.
Life shall end captured a slave.
Most are slaves to life, such bitter end.
Only heal a heart so broken, let it mend.
Capture time, watch a minute, seems so long.
Love a life now singing any new song.
Never turn bitter, pain life so sore vexed.
Close never your book so many more pages shall come next.
Live a dream, never letting go while they exist.
Close your eyes over a waterfall, feel a spirit in a mist.
Saving only a dance shall never last.
Only a man having no memories, never had any past.
Awakening suddenly from walking dead.
So much in a road, many miles ahead.
Life shall never in a lifetime be explained.
Only ending death has one gained.
Enjoy life into a canyon why such bewilderment eyes.
Dancing in your dream, western skies.
Life never confuse many trails, affliction seems torment.
Treasure little things,
A spirit dancing against my wind, honeysuckle scent.
Open your window feeling four seasons.
Life going stale, explain now reason.
Never any glass house shattered any dream.
When any spirit captures your dream,
Hold on in your mind to deem.
Locked in a mind, separating voices from reality.
Separating men from a world from brutality.

Maybe in your life never taking heed has no notice.
Hold life sacred it is not a water lily white lotus.
Reach out holding on from all Sea's looking troubled.
Give life only chance never will be doubled.

Cold Rains

Death knocks on a door.
Too tired to pick my bones up off the floor.
Standing now numb in pouring cold rain.
Scream in the night no more pain.
Death covers my eyes as I fall to the ground.
My Spirit leaves my body no more sound.
Lifeless & breathless not yet done.
Spirit consumes me, warms my body as morning sun.
I wave good-bye to Great Spirit shining northern skies.
Night, world stops turning, night cold rains my Spirit cries.
So I be out of my head.
In house, living dead.
I shall never forget cold rain cloudy skies, Spirit so bright.
This dark cold night I lost will, won this fight.
Say I snapped my fingers.
Pneumonia left this body no more choir singers.
Then, as now, I know what I seen.
Spirit leaving my body now with meaning what life means.

Cornblossom

Over 100 men women children died.
Only Hawk whispering pines now cried.
Stonewall faces.
Grace to disgrace.
Jacob Soldier died warrior scalp he lost.
His family love life dues cost.
Garden seed of love, Cornblossom.
Never forget first sign spring blossoms.
What must live what must die.
When a Hawk to the pines cry.
What does die must live.
Are we dead are we alive?

Fenced Desires

Death shadows beauty to die, for let Dark Angel just taste.
Death shall end so many years, missed never recycled waste.
Standing hidden behind Angel's fence.
Opportunity passed opportunity missed crying make sense.
100 lost years one now shall tarry.
Away from thought pieces paper to marry.
Leaving life only behind cold lonely bars.
Spirits set free drinking whiskey from jars.
Exhausting words making pleasure consumed.
Until burning more fires destiny assumed.
Pinned, fence, death no place to run.
Moon shadows killed darkness covering sun.
Taste new life soft skin to lick.
Light a candle burn from both ends wick.
Wearing unto grave, long flowing black veil.
Never before tasting pleasure sweet stripping hell.
Dreaming sweet fantasy never lived now lost.
Priceless memories only few come no cost.
Justify lust man made morals.
Eating forbidden fruits, bed, ocean soaked corals.
Remove far from myth man made lies.
Making love on cloud nine heavenly skies.
Climbing Angel's stairs worship her temple.
Taste new life all over tongue massage made simple.
Forbidden fears only one missed.
Stealing mere memories, two bodies never kissed.
Broken silence hear any wolf growl.
Remove Angel's halo, now comes shrieking howl.
Memories consumed draining sand lost time.
When to naked bodies dance makes wind chimes.

Wages, death, memories gone, just garnish.
New shinning life in your mouth, taste silver only to tarnish.
Enjoyment falls released never life mistaking.
Goes beyond life now spanking.
Now to walk your fears into my ocean shaky plank.
Burning violins or any dancing fiddles.
Still being same singing life with new riddles.
So taste morals blood poisoned, lost free in any river to flow.
Watch thrusting rocket eye caught brief show.
Now built new bridge closed your gap.
When two naked bodies entwine, making love legs wrap.

Death Before Death

Many has seen death before death
In their dead lives many shall not
Find life until death to live.
Right hand you hold death, the left hand life
Which shall prevail. Left shall only prevail when
In life they live unto death to live.
Many that live are dead.
Many that are dead are yet alive.
What will haunt one is not to die yet to live,
When dead are they alive?
I brought life to your closed eyes
Would you then fear death to life or life to death.

Getchamagoo

How shall one be away though be within?
How shall we be within but be away?
The Moon shall rise, then fall asleep on his back in his own will
In our own living then sleeping world
As we pass from one world unto another.
One can do everything then still please no man,
Man can do nothing unto the children
Then please every child in the smallest ways.
Every man must pass by the way of the child
Before he must journey on
Before man gets stuck unto his own world.
Man must search his own religion to follow after no man.
Only a man can carry one up on top of the mountain though.
Man must stand on his own accordance,
For man must stand alone.
Then face the wind on his own mountain.
Through the hills of Gethchamagoo
In the faint distance a owl whispers who,
Who do you be? Who are you?
To search with eyes closed, wide open.

Goyathalay

Goyathalay Goyathalay Goyathalay Goyathalay
Goyathalay Goyathalay Goyathalay
Let us race the wind.
Higher, higher to skies end.
You rode the white night, now ride black cloud.
Let us go home, away from this crowd.
Matters not what man has called.
When wind whispers your name in the fall.
We may look different blood still red.
Hearts, we left for the dead.
I felt your pain as cold winter pines cry.
I shed no more tears, my skin is dry.
One day circle life complete.
Let us watch these men compete.
Goyathalay Goyathalay Goyathalay Goyathalay
Goyathalay Goyathalay Goyathalay
Your name shall live forever.
Your home never to end Gila River.
There name be on papers, soon forgotten.
Your heart I never forgot.
They call this civilization.
In world mockery courts civil.
Let them keep their pain new drugs.
While we sleep on deer skin rugs.

Life

Born in thy wrong lifetime, in thy wrong era.
Been lost thy whole lifetime, looking for home.
Like a last flower petal fallen dancing on thy wind.
Freely let my limbs dangle to & fro
Free to go across a forbidden land.
Sun darkens my skin bronze again
Glistening in thy golden sun ray.
Spirit water drips from upon my temple
Crashing unto virgin soil.
Animals of thy forest Sleep,
Feed and protect me.
Birds awake me with new song let us talk.
Wolf whispers good night as thy bison listen unto thy horse.
Shhh, silence unto thy night.
In thy man race of life we are lost for we been found.
Every man shall lose his glory in thy morning,
Dance lost on thy wind.
Only voice to hear in thy wind my family my children.
Give me a home wild flower garden on top a mountain.
Feel thy breath,
Hear thy voice,
Morning sun warm my bones awake me.
Every morning with a warm smile.
Meet me again mountain in thy sky.

River to No Return

Pouring her troubles in a river never.
Her dam is built,
She can't hold burdens behind any lever.
One day heavy rains came,
Behind her dam raging her flood.
When mercury busted now,
Contaminated blood.
Racing to a sea no return.
Reading her story one page shall turn.
Asked her now to read to finish her book.
Leaving mere men bewildered look.
Time standing still in her river boat's crash.
When in pain, teeth shall be razors now slash.
Never shall flood gates shut contain.
Raging river of tears called pain.
Running troubles rushing whirlpool.
Not all can swim without help, never a fool.
Sailing Mother's ocean never fret.
Helping hands never regret.
Rain dance stops, rain dove sings.
Mother's love beneath her wings.
Crying never what one can understand.
Joining hands united we shall stand.

Spirit Child of Morning Light

"WE ARE NOT CONQUERED YET
REMEMBER MY CHILDREN
REMEMBER MY PEOPLE"
PRINCESS CORNBLOSSOM LAST WORDS

Remember this in prayer when alone.
Iron Eyes hearts turn unto stone.
What has been only days yet to come.
Price unto death, only price again pay some.
One changes not history,
We just live history over falling waterfalls.
Say this unto tear Spirits cry unto hearts all.
Spirit dwells within right from wrong.
When birds awaken with old love song.
Remember fallen Spirit child of morning light.
As mourning star disappears from sight.

Death Shadows

Thy Rhyme, Thy Riddle.
Thy man in thus middle.
Thy live, Thy die,
Thy laugh, Thy cry,
Thy rock thus build.
Thy gun thus wield.
Thy child played.
Thy child prayed.
Thy rising sun.
Thy killing gun.
Thy rises Thy East.
Thy man beget Thy beast.
Thy oily hands,
Thy vanishing sands
Why beget thus same?
Thy life game,
Thy sky thus blue,
Thy life clue.
Thy rides Thy Gray Shadow.
Thy opens Thy death window.
Thy changed Thy seed thus corn.
Thy still thus be born.
Thy song bird mourning.
Thy fog lifted thus morning.

House of Pain

World pain, in house pain.
Bad medicine, bad religion, for the vain.
Numb to a world a world to numb.
Black eyes, black thumbs.
Worst mistake being born.
No whiskey, No pain, No white corn.
Trick or treat, so trick our minds.
Any day, any time, another day pain finds.
Dead men walking.
Look no one is talking.
In due time another dam breaks.
Tears go dry in the heart lakes.
None too soon this day closes.
Black eye beans Mary of Roses.
Return me to an innocent womb.
Away from house of shattered tombs.

Lil Angel Spoken

As My Spirit Passes Over A Lil Angel.
In A World Seems So Tangled.
A Tear I Catch In My Hand.
Taking Away Angels Pain, He Will Withstand.
Giving Angel Hope Now Looking Into The Soul,
His Blue Eyes.
As Now Small Teardrops Dries.
The Darkness Shines Now A Moon Bow.
Under The Stars A Scarce Show.
Tears Flowing Over A Rushing Water Fall.
Her Moon Bow Shines from the Downfall.
A Life So Fought New Sunshine Breaks A Storm.
Standing Tall, Taking New Form.
As The Dark Angel Carried Her Up The Mountain So Steep.
Now Her Sunshine Shines Now On Children Giving
A Fresh Drink, As She So Weeps
Lil Children Shall Look Upwards
Seeking Guidance In Soft Spoken Words.

Mark of the Beast

Graves behind Fort, you gave to protect.
Elite to desecrate you select.
Not you hair, skull, femur bone & horse tack.
Why Geronimo or Harlyn cries you will not back.
So money buys your power.
God damn clock tower.
Thoughts to protect land of the brave.
1910 dig up another grave.
Does only your Apache helicopter get attention.
The real Apache you never mention.
So I am your enemy, one you hate.
Old gold tooth silver plate.
Words today few to say.
Real life not all games we play.
Apache tear I hold comes from days being old.
Still clear as ever seeing through black gold.
Now comes real life dues.
Repent will not just do.
To wear 322 mark of the beast.
Eating your Sunday feast.
My name you gave only Danny.
My grave I dig besides my granny.
Birds of Paradise again one day bloom.
Far away from games of doom.
My lips shall never cease.
Rest in peace.

Pale Face

Only a body now a face being pale.
Now days weak, ones become frail.
Deep into eyes sky blue.
A time on shall be gone without any clue.
Slew from a poison a reaper infected.
When our world turns no more life rejected.
Destiny never owned purchased wealth.
Even when strong men shall lose his health.
High tide shall wash away prints left be any foot.
Faster now a falling star shall shoot.
All men created equal to be seen like a star.
Now pain be gone leaving a marked scar.
Let not tears fall a cold rain.
As Death Reaper has slain.
Now pains taken away feeling in paradise city.
Never feel pain, never give joy from pity.
A dream is only a dream, look for a memory cherished.
Our memory more than a dream we finished.

Angel's Cup Life

Angles journey not a barren waste land.
Delicate touch, Angel's soft hand.
Touching many hearts on many highways.
Even crossing a few rocky bridges.
On angels journey atop the mountain ridge.
Angels glowing shinny bright light.
Pierced through Angels darkest night.
Falling several times, climbing up.
Holding now in Angels hands life in a cup.
Cup never running dry.
As Angels starting to cry.
Runneth thee cup over, now come drink.
Reaching higher now, not on the brink.
Misery, Pain, Sickness, Tainted hearts,
does not set one worlds apart.
Defying the laws only from Mother Nature.
All else Destiny hold strong with good stature.

Life

Life is not a card game one so deals.
Eat the meat makes tasty meals.
Times corrupt never Animals, times two.
Everyone money greedy there law to sue.
Even the cunning fox escapes to the den.
Newborn any no one left to defend.
Scream my morals are bad,
When yours are more sad.
Leaving the animals to defend the baby,
Innocent so tearful not a maybe.
Defend a country, defend the innocent.
Goes beyond prayer and repent.
Learning from our past.
This life shall never last.
Eternity on earth define it.
Taking a horse by the bit.
Will guide the journey as one will travel.
Look upon not me so bedazzled or puzzled.
For the voices are not real.
Treasure life to never steal.
Take my story as you will.
Life is not just – let's make a deal.

Spirit in the Dark

Heart center mark.
Four stars align.
Begin open sign.
Awaken living rock.
Spirit start clock.
Spirit wind down neck.
In temple doom wreck.
Consume us, heal those weak,
Only to those who seek
Whispers.

Spirit of Ancestors

Cold night I die.
Moon shut his eyes to cry.
All once was good.
Days left hunting home alone now he stood,
Crumbling to his knees.
Cold winter night, tear drops freeze.
Ground frozen red where his family now lay.
Wind not a word to say.
Return me to dark moon, my mother's womb.
Unearthed dirt bare bloody hands, family tomb.
Squeeze blood from dirt frozen weary hands,
Screaming his spirit to farthest lands.
Body now weak blanket tomb for days.
Prisoner to land leaves his heart behind, forgotten ways.
We cannot live in the past.
Lest we forget we will be the last.
They given their war memorial.
Take away children memorials.
I lift my hands to a moon.
Wipe bloody tears from red sky afternoon.

Frozen In Time

Frozen 1800 year old cowboy,
Froze in 20th century rock.
Free to roam free range dirty socks.
Give us land, come and go free lost tumble weed.
Government mule done dirt cheap.
Games forgotten, now we only frog leap.
Given land keep what is underneath.
Never stop stealing minerals beneath.
Now new disease fills our body, our air.
Water dirty taxed fare.
Keep the land spirits, dance free.
Salty dog, salty sea.
Fill land, full cows.
Broken plows.
Spirits cloak sky far as you can see.
Life to own life to kill spirits now free.

Snows long ago

Eyes that cry no tears that fall.
Spirit that mourns, no words to sound.
Bones that are cold no fire to warm.
Mirror reflects no reflections to shine.
Days that are endless, weeks that slip by.
Strength then comes, then leaves on the wind.
Prayers to pray, wisdom to seek.
Days weightless, Days lifeless, Days meaningless.
Winter awakes, moon hidden night.
Lips that dry to sing.
Wind that sings ends in a howl.
Soft snow begins to fall dreams yet begin.
Snow fills my eyes,
listening to the night sky cry.
My heart melts snow in my hand.
In these snow tracks I stand.
Crackling campfire, sing me to sleep.
Long ago snows so deep.
Red cedar, soft needle bed.
Spirit of the snow we will go.
Out the mouth Spirit will blow.
Ancient land of the whitest snows.

O'Death

Eyes Called Death, O'Death
Into the eyes death's cold stare.
Look into the center light now glare.
Hollow as the soul, now empties.
Death riddles the hillsides, so many cemeteries.
As a hand dealt, death shall fall,
A voice sounding when at death's call.
A life stalking in the belly comes death binding.
As death shall rattle, not as teeth grinding.
Spirit letting go, face now shallow ghost.
Now dancing as a mother's host.
Now before one shall accept.
Shed no tears as one is summons to hell never swept.
As the body shall be left, to feed the worms to nourish.
Starting a cycle as Mother Nature shall flourish.
Clean a trumpet made from brass.
As children come tomorrow to a mass.
Take my ashes send them to heaven or hell.
When you hear not a trumpet, only a bell.
I'll never cry O'Death take me home.
Even after death come and gone.
My soul lead me down many happy trails.
Even days strength left frail.
Fear not Death, only when a friend shall befriend.
Mix my ashes as Mother Earth's shall mend.

River

River, carry me away,
Lift me up to the clouds.
Fly on the wings of a hawk.
Heart circle dances in the sky.
Low lying fog, cover my eyes.
Lift from your breath.
Disappear in your bosom.
Your warm eyes open in the east.
Climbing above the mountains,
Stairways to your heart,
Your rock face, soft skin,
Gentle Spirit in your voice.
Birds sing as children.
Bring life to the songbirds.
Tree sways as lost in a dream.
From your soft breath,
New cycle life awakes.
From your cold hands,
Warm heart begins spring.

On The Wind

Let me take your pain away.
I will hold your troubles.
In my hands, so tight.
Carry it up so high.
Stairway Mountain.
Turn them loose.
Burdens and troubles.
On the wind.
Carried far away.
Never return.
Pain now gone.
Troubles released.
Return to home.
Heal now feel.
What it is to be free.
On the wind.
Burdens and troubles.
Move our bodies.
We are healed.

War

All these killings in war,
To kill one another.
Everyone loses something,
What we must gain.
My best friend is a Hawk,
No one understands our talk.
Flying by sitting in a tree.
Not screaming at you,
For our world one day will end.
Gather herbs, drinking tea.
Dancing in the night sky.
Spirits on the wind.
We all bleed red.
Every breed that breathes.
Even a tree will bleed.
War battles to the end.
Death to one victory to another.
Part of life with a face.
Before we are Spirits on the wind.
Racing to the northern lights.
Dancing in the end.

Love

To My Family Roberts

I speak your name Tyler.
In the mountains you were born.
Brothers and sister on a mountain.
Beyond Oil Valley.
Crosscut wood before winter.
Mule snaking logs.
Chickens and hogs.
Water from a spring.
Down below your home.
Gardens and wood cook stove.
Memories take me home.
Milk from a cow.
Brother John and sister Polly.
Brothers Columbus and Cas.
Tyler went home.
With brother Liscoe.
Jr their first born.
Father Luther.
Mother Lula.
Wayne County, Kentucky.

Slow Dance

Searching to steal the night again,
Lady in red.
Slowly the dance commences,
Sing the stars to sleep.
Breath winter chill wake me,
This winter night, soft snow tracks.
Take me back in time,
Dancing counter clockwise.
Take my breath away,
Dancing while the moon sleeps.
Warm us soft blanket of clouds.
Our dance, no one to ever steal away.
Naked trees sway so gently.
Take our breath away.
Give new life to the fallen star.
Memories that pierced this dark night.
Wolf eyes watch to steal this kiss again.
Memories of the slow dance, begins the snow.

Candy Heart

Passing out Lil candy Hearts.
On a day even worlds set Apart.
Sending a heart with a big ole Hugs.
In virtual world, so forget about the ones who Bugs.
On a day looking for only warm Smiles.
Only running many country Miles.
Sending many little hearts called an Angel.
For even knowing you not in a web, we did Tangle.
Sending out Lil heart to all called so Fine.
So my biggest treasure your all Angel's called Mine.
Sending out a Lil heart a name one called Magic.
In a world away from pain called one Tragic.
Take not away a Lil candy heart called Love Life.
In a world fighting against evil Strife.
Never to last cherish a Lil heart called First Kiss.
Never regret what memories never to Miss.
Sending out even more Lil hearts called All Star.
Love from even darkness can heal even a dark Scar.
Never forget the many Lil hearts eating called Awesome.
For a beauty many flowers in large meadows will Blossom.
Eating Lil candy hearts named my Way.
Treasure all to treasure one another so treasure Today.
Sorry guys my last candy heart is not going to You.
Though cheers pop a top here is some strong Mountain Dew.
To the Angels take my last candy Heart Kiss Me.
When two souls now are set Free.

Love Song

Will you sing a new love song.
I will sing a new love song.
We will sing a new love song.
From our heart we all belong.
We are all someone singing,
A new love song, a new love song

Brothers

Bub will one day ride again.
When he gets tired of his new love.
Four wheel toy never be like a horse.
Saddle sores don't hurt no more.
When you find a saddle that fits,
Leather bridle, metal bits.
Four by four throwing fits.
Horse eating grass, cheaper than gas.
Horse camp, nights cold and damp.
Stuck in the mud on the other side of the fence.
Growing old riding horses again.
Flood now stopped river out the banks.
Charlie gone floating way down the creek.
Boots feet not wet, Charlie will swim.
On the other side two brother just grin.
Hillbilly, Pepper stands Black Cloud.
Stevie racing through the corn.
Black Cloud done at the end.
Before the rain comes back around.
Now the darkness has come.
Come back around on this merry go of life.
War cries Hyden time now flies.
Where brothers are found.

New Season United Love

I shall wear black until end.
Darkness we hold inside us men.
My light shines through unto end.
Women future children to defend.
We never change our teachings.
Honor misleading preachings.
Thy be One Great Spirit, one God.
Same love same chastising rod.
We are consumed, fiery mistakes.
Every living body breaks.
Every living Spirit one day smiles.
Country roads take me back that country mile.
As Crow shall fly.
Great Spirit Hawk to cry.
Eagle again flies, proud and free.
Away from yester year, raging sea.
Apache Nation through hills unto Cherokee Nation.
Across seven seas united relations.
Seed shall perish away from hand in hand united.
Before disasters, fiery love ignited.
What man harbors torch greed.
We live, we love we all red bleed.
Living Spirits again shall rise.
In temple educated Owl wise.
Death takes death to shaky hand.
Land owns man never man the land.
He may conquer this mountain.
Why he never found youth fountain.
This new season united love.
As sun shines from above.

Summer Nights

Summer grew shorter with his cold heart.
Breaking heat waves with his cool breath.
Sun sets awaken his soft rough touch.
Clothe me in darkness, her soft skin to caress.
Her warm breathe down my naked chest.
Summer night breaks silence, screeching frog.
Voice Screech Owl breaks silence her shrill.
Set me free, breaking bondage sands o' time.
Lovers of the fallen night, fog dew drops as soft rain.
Abandoned Castles in the sky reclaimed full of life.

Her Mountains

To climb her mountains.
Looking for youth fountains.
Her skin soft to touch.
Behind her scars painful such.
Her breath she breathes.
Changing fall leaves.
Fruit forbidden.
Secret caves hidden.
This what heart brings.
Drinking from seven springs.
In corner no longer father sits.
Butterfly mitts.
New dawn, we live.
Our hearts we give.
Every breath we take,
Filled so many mistakes.
Perfection only the end.
When no more rivers bend.
No more to climb mountains.
Searching youth fountains.
So give today.
Tomorrow, we will play.

Tonight Feel My Spirit a Warm Touch

As I lay down on cold ground to kiss ground
Breathing my warm Spirit love
Warming the ground comes over us.
I will whisper the Spirit love song into the wind.
Love my brother as no other,
Love my life as first day as newlywed wife.
Spreading love to four corners,
As cross roads, we cross our heart.
Golden love in Spirit love that shall dance,
A new love song, an eternity.
Many shall pass through in our life the same moon.
Love song life dance,
We shall dance with stars again one night soon.
We talk to the tree life,
It will not move we sing to tree life this love song life,
Then tree will dance with us in Spirit of the wind,
A new love song life.

Love and Hate

Words from Love to Hate.
Roads travelled open a Debate.
Flesh & Bones returning to Dust.
Only a desire drives love to Lust.
All so different being the Same.
Hate one needs to Blame.
So different, we all hate Something.
Expressing reproach no need Admonishing.
None walks same foot-steps so Trace.
Pushing death finding destiny an ending Race.
Never to hate or love is never Wrong.
Battles – Tribulations a journey made Long.
Shapes a Spirit then a Mind.
All so different the end Death shall Find.

You Will Heal

When you can't feel.
You will heal.
Go ahead just break free.
You are so free.
What you can't see.
Now you will see.
Ears shall open.
To sound fallen tears.
This cleanses now heals your Spirit.
When you can't feel.
You will heal.

Forbidden Treasures

As he was not a boy when he took her Hand.
His claws leaves her soul with a new Brand.
Taking life not to death as a Dream.
Waking now hear her Scream.
Lust only runs onto as sun parched Soil.
Now Her Moisture So Drips,
To moisten sun parched Lips.
Glow coming not from tender Youth,
Watching, observing she now secretly Sleuth.
As her animals comes from distinctive Nature.
Open new roads to a new Future.
Taking her youth she now drinks new Flavors,
In her mouth tongue licking new Savors.
For an enjoyment drinking his Pleasure,
Life yet tried secret Treasure.
As a lightning Rod burning Finger Tips,
Grinding forcing sudden Trips.
As the rod is ground buries deep in her Tenderness.
Invading Angel's forbidden locked Fortress.
Touching a shock from the tip of the Stake.
As sweet love they so make the earth Quake.
Come now feeling the Aftershock.
She shall now never Mock.
Waking from not wet dreams in hidden Bed Rooms.
Into a crowded street thunder Booms.

I Ride My Pony

I ride my pony,
I ride my pony fast.
I ride my pony,
I ride my pony slow.
I ride my pony,
I ride my pony where no other man will go.
I ride my pony,
I ride my pony up these hills.
I ride my pony,
I ride my pony down this bluff.
I ride my pony,
I ride my pony he is tough.
I ride my pony,
I ride my pony where rivers end and the land begins.
I ride my pony,
I ride my pony Mache.

Mother's Warmth

Listen now as my flute now talks.
Going to miss these long walks.
No more going around any river bend.
Listening to Mother whisper with the wind.
Even the little things we often take for granted.
In Mother's forest treasures enchanted.
Going to miss mother's blooming forest.
When Redbuds then Dogwoods florist.
For A Mother that grows such beauty to watch.
Never forget the smell green pines one calls Scotch.
Inner peace from perfect rhythm, listen to ragging water.
Watching a Mother put back what men do slaughter.
I have been caught many times in Mother's rain.
Spring time air so fresh after a shower
No one ever captured a sweet smell to contain.
Looking upon Mother's Castle, beautiful walls solid stone.
Men trying to Conquer Mother's Castle Walls, never to own.
Into a belly a Mother's dark caves walls magnificent.
Returning to a Mother now a descendant.
When my ashes scattered return to form.
Even as dust Mother shall open her eye
From the west to feel her love warm.
As Mother's sand shall disappear from under my feet.
Going to now miss the beauty from the outside such a treat.

Mother's Brook

Though our Spirits only did touch in a mist.
Angel's soul touched an Iron Fist.
Turning water not into bitter wine.
Even a drunkard recalls pain running with swine.
Treasure in a life more than any price.
Do not try to convert me to Christ.
Some a Christ they so seek.
Calling Darkness even sleek.
To feel a smiles warm soft Glow.
A Religion I only Bestow.
Even a Vulture shall smell Rotten flesh before it shall see.
So eat not with Vultures fill from a life a Blooming Tree.
Open your eyes in a Land Good & Evil.
I shall be good to the good more Evil to the Weasel.
My ways Good or Evil shall always be in store.
This firm ground I tread even on Eastern Sea Shores.
So pour my ashes back on Mother Earth.
Then I will return to my Birth.
Only putting back what I took.
Now running fast again in Mothers Brook.

Mother's Love

A Mother will always be watching over her baby.
Even as they grow, no matter what they do no maybe.
A friend none like a Mother's Love,
Will always hold one gentle like holding a Turtle Dove.
As the baby grows when starting to walk,
Mumbling lil words starting to talk.
Even in life while one walks on Mother Earth.
Her love only started from the baby's Birth.
So when one stumbles then falls.
Open up to the true friend,
The one who runs to your beacon calls.
For the time on Mother Earth shall be limited.
Though a Mothers love has no boundaries, unlimited.
For many show there face acting like a friend who care.
Though many will hide in the shadows
When burdens are not bare.
Loving Mother's eyes never will hide.
Even in the storm on high tide.
Listen to the Mother's soft voice as she speaks.
Her Love shall teach never a school that swims bleak.

Wind Chimes

Sometimes I wonder why we ever crossed paths.
We are like the abandoned old house
Our bones one day go back to the soil as dirt.
Even in our difference know still I love you,
For it is better to be loved,
Than never loved at all once spoken.
Maybe one day we shall go on a long walk together again,
For we cannot make no promises of the future,
For we only love today.
Then today let me speak love that I still love you all.
Part my Spirit cries, I run and hide.
It follows me like my shadows.
For some my ancestors they say,
They know not where they come from.
It is like a hole in my spirit,
That cries to a Hawk unto a Eagle.
Then harsh words man makes your heart even more sad,
Like we are not of human form,
As they are, for we do not know where we belong.
Today, as of yesterday, I resend my love as token peace.
For we are at enough war even amongst ourselves.
It shall not change day or night.
Only how we shall live in our last days in harmony.
So let our lips sing only words from love.
For our creator blessed us to share this day.
In the sun on the mountain once again,
As once in the beginning.
We are free in the wind on a mountain,
As wind chimes.

Midnight Lovers

Take me to road of Sweet desires.
As adrenaline rushes, taking breathe like burning fires.
Jump this bridge taking our breath away.
Bite my neck, taste my flesh.
Her Breast sweet as the honey Dew so fresh.
New passion, Now be replenished.
So many trips in a Fantasy left unfinished.
In a wilderness never scared, Marking territory New.
As a hungry wolf shall stalk then slew.
As her mouths waters for a New treasure.
Gold searching not her pleasure.
Taking her stake made now tarnished silver.
Dipping in His cold soul as a rushing Winter river.
Hunger growing every day, a mind infected.
As her glow into his eyes, that dark night reflected.
Devouring him, taking her time as a falling moon.
Then taking charge, laying her head off a cliff head so swoon.
As the rushing river of blood rushes to her brain,
As he drives his stake deep in her cavern pulling her mane.
Claws he digs into her holds her firm on edge.
For a naked bed high on a cliff's ledge.
Eating her alive as a starving wolf shall feed.
Licking her tender dripping lips with his greed.
As her weakness makes her sweat.
Her tender loins sweet, so wet.
The fragrance fills the night air.
As her teeth digging into fresh meat so tear.
When the whippoorwill sings with excitement.
Her hormones raging new incitement.
As she jumps to her feet around hips wrapping her legs.

Wolf now howls never to beg.
For using his strength to control her body.
For making love as fine art even abstract embody.
As the bodies mold as one came shaft working vigorously.
A faith he worshiped her tender body rigorously.
Night died so fast as sun awoke to kill the stars,
As a body mended from old scars.

Ah Victory

Every touch burning fires his desires.
Wolf Moon heart beat tune.
Written word day shall be lived.
From finger tip flames truth.
Animal instinct dark passion.
Burn day unto night search.
Deep in his Spirit east within.
Hidden chambers 223 time.
For thy glory in face paint.
Light bleeds into dark.
V for victory conquer mountain.

One Day

One day God, Creator looked down,
Then smiled my son your legs look
Tired then weary know my son.
I made all creation unto man to look
After to use, learn then talk to.
Then let the four legged become your best
Friend he will carry all your burdens.
And weary troubles away into the
Sunset to forget hidden deep in the
Stars tonight.

Shadow Dancer

Shadow dancer, dance with me tonight.
Dance with me in the pouring rain.
Light show, light our dance floor.
Draw night hold me tight in your arms.
Spin us around, follow the shadow.
Earth is turning, heart beating,
Light foot dance floor rumbles.
Flashing talking hands, bare feet,
Walking silk flower petals.
Breathe new breath softly upon my lips.
Breath taken new Spring dance begins.
Moon sleeps in his dream.
Warm clouds dance across the sky.
Wake me not from this dream.
Eyes from the north.
Sleeping ram naked be.
Dancing shadows.

Nature

3 Butterfly Kisses

3 Butterfly kisses.
Dance on the clouds.
Blow softly wind.
Across her tender hands.
Refresh her delicate face.
Let her new strength grow.
Grow from within.
For faith was made on a mountain.
Then seed from doubt planted in the valley.
Believe in thine self.
Then shall you stand in the wind on the mountain.

I am...Sometimes

I am as the water.
Sometimes soft,
Sometimes cold,
Sometimes troubled,
Sometimes calm,
Sometimes relaxing,
Sometimes revitalizing,
Sometimes healing,
Sometimes rough,
Sometimes fallen,
Sometimes lost.

Light to Night, Night to Light

Skies are Light turn unto Night.
Thunder shall rumble, no cloud in the sky.
Tears from the Heavens cry.
Birds and Animals run then hide.
Man-made River forks narrow now wide.
Earthen Stairway rises to the cloud.
Falls to bury standing crowd.
Total darkness Night returns unto Light.
Corn returned unto stone.
Sparkling crystal the sand return to tears.
Sparkle in the eye of man, his Spirit.

Sea Shell

Hold you in my hands as a sea shell from the sea.
Heart beat the drum in my ear listen.
Castle in the sky rolls by.
Power in the wooden staff whom carries Flute song of love,
To connect to the Hawk the Eagle unto God, our Creator.
To play with our Spirit unto Spirit.
Sound from the wind carries our Spirit from the sea.
Same feathers for a world to taste.
Warrior to love, Warrior to fight, Warrior whispers good night.

Wild Flowers

Here comes the rain.
Why do we have pain?
Why do we hurt?
For our family, our friend.
Wind blows strong to only lay.
Comforting words to say.
Pick up our family, our friend.
Listen gentle blows the wind.
Scent from fresh cut flowers.
Dancing on the wind butterfly.
Night broke silence wolf not to cry.
Power to heal delicate flower.
Even a wild flower needs rest.
Only flower to bloom an eternity.
Firefly shines upon beauty.
Gathering flowers in my heart.
For our family, our friend.
Moon halo shines upon thee.
Reflections cast from the sea.
Gathering wild flowers tonight.
Darkest hour before light.
Good night whispers the wind.
Broken hearts, broken bones mend.

Winter Howl

Cold stare from his dark wolf eyes.
Sends the moon to his shadows.
For he is hungry tonight in need of fresh meat.
His song from his Spirit silences the night.
Cold breath, open her locked windows hidden desires.
Wolf claws rasp against her stone walls.
Stars now hide their eyes.
White now yellow sparks fly.
Claws rasp her tender skin,
His fangs bite into her soft neck.
She feels his heart beat in his vein upon his temple.
Tomb from blue river slate, she lays life less.
His shadow as he stands hides her innocence,
For she lost the battle this dark night.
Holding only another memory in the broken hour glass.
Clasping two tufts of his fur.

Wolf Moon

This is a new dawning night meet me under a Wolf Moon.
Heartbeats stop heartbeats race no other night to soon.
January cold sweats warm our touch.
New Year starts routine no such.
Soft snow our blanket we walk on.
Steam from our bodies, hot breath smoke,
Innocent lost new dawn.
Live to regret.
Snow now stops up it let.
Security blanket of solitude.
Crickets this cold night awaken not as our violins are burning.
Only one world away this night,
Our Wolf Moon worlds did stop turning.

Buffalo Dance

I seen a Butterfly with broken wings.
Lifted her delicate body to the sky.
Told her let the wind help her fly.
Seen wounded Hawk carried him all my life.
His claw seers my heart.
Mighty bison fell at my feet.
First told him I know now, go home.
As watched a Mustang stumble then fall,
Breaking his leg.
Told him go home racing the wind.
Unto thy stars end.
Carrying Silver Wing Dancer in my bosom.
As we stumble & tumble through this life.
Unto our home in thus Sky.
Where Buffalo dance rumble the clouds.
Ground rumbles under our feet.

Another Butterfly

Hide me away my Spirit from pains.
Silent tears ink stains.
Butterfly wishes.
Butterfly color fishes.
Gardens eternity bloom again.
Carry this Spirit thus journey we began.
Sky our home.
Freely spirit horses roam.
Blanket us in stars.
Atop thus mountain afar.
Spirit wind now blows.
Gentle from east shoals.
Flutter dancing wind.
Hide me unto the end.

Butterfly Dancer

Queen of the meadow.
Butterfly window.
Golden Sun Flowers Golden.
Cedar holden.
Doe deer.
Turkey peer.
Heart soft.
Rock loft.
Butterfly.
Clear sky.
Soft touch.
Flower bunch.
Bee few.
Silver wing crew.
Hawk fly different two.
Eagle fast.
Youth past.
Turtle grand.
Tender hand.
Dancing wings.
Heart sings.
Butterfly capable to travel.
Thy sea thy highest,
Mountains to shine,
Tender beauty dancing,
Golden skies, golden flowers.
Powerful tender heart touching,
Power as thy Butterfly dances in thy wind,
Unto thy end singing grace.

Let your fingers dance softly in thy wind,
With grace as Butterfly dancing.
In thy wind thine besought thy Butterfly Dancer.
Butterfly searches four corners four winds,
To Shine thy tender beauty.
Dancing grace in thus wind.
All creation looks upon thus beauty,
With power to connect two worlds.
Thy Butterfly Dancer in thine wind.
Sing I am thy Butterfly Dancer,
Dancing in thy wind.
Come dance with me,
For thy whole world to see.
Dancing in thy four winds,
Dancing unto thy end.
Butterfly wings skin velvet,.
Dance flutter in the wind.
I hear dance soft.
As wings sing love song life,
Sweet dreamsssssssssssssssssssssssss.
Hugs, kiss.

Butterflies and Bees,
Love and Spirituality in Little Animals

Today sun shine,
And warm us.
Blue sky,
Went like few,
Same place where I saw a Bird of Prey.
And a green Lizard.
Today heard the warm sound of the bees, Bees,
Dancing on Rose of Mary on Flowers.
Smell Nature.
Quiet walk.
Sun warmed my body and my spirit,
Better feeling than in a sea.
Saw Many white and yellow Butterflies,
Dancing and flying together.
Saw a sort of bee,
With a warm sound and many smiles in his wings.
Smiles were in Nature,
Warm too,
Love too.
Feel spirituality in little animals today.

Clouds

I lift my hands higher to the sky.
Why there cold so dry?
Asking many questions,
Tell me no lies.
Why so cold and dry?
Answers under the sky.
Walking on clouds above men.
Looking for no hearts to win.
Today racing by no end.
Another voice in the wind.
Why there cold so dry?
Children in garden water.
Ancient voices in wind speak.
Tears dried away.
Golden sun ray.
Men fade as sun man made weak.
Golden path turned away.
Clouds dark then gray,
Children of Mother Earth,
Returning unto birth,
Race the wind ride Black Cloud.
Make us humble not so proud.

Dark Wings

Proud as a bear,
My friend I care.
Dark Wings, Dark Wings,
Mending my heart sings.
Let us be calm as we talk.
Know my Spirit as a Hawk.
My hands are rough.
Your days been tough.
I see the living Spirit in your eye.
As my Spirit for you shall cry.
Days been long.
All went wrong.
My friend be strong.
As mending hearts.
Let us give life another start.
Before unto our womb we return.
Open our eyes make our head turn.
To Northern Skies.
My friend again flies.
Another Bird of Paradise.
Ask an Owl so wise.
An Eagle Prayer so loud.
Uplifting this Black Cloud.

House of the Panther

Shadows followed him to a house of the Panther.
Through Eight Fingers,
Across Hells bridge to the Devil's chair.
His eyes laid wait like a cold fog stare.
In this valley, Kings cries echo to a stone wall.
Knock on the door hide in the house Spirits call.
Spirits again run free & wild as the deer.
What is this man you fear?
Satisfied only in the eye of man.
Spirits hunger for more old rusty tin can.
Eyes now open unto man three parts.
Mind, our brain, we trick and train from the start.
Body is water, cells and dirt from the beginning.
Spirits our destiny or our uncanny ending.

Enchanted Sea

Many shall never see.
Sea so enchanted.
Eagle eye slanted.
Piercing unto hearts of love.
Hearts as pure as first snow dove.
Dreams for every glistening star,
Shall two Spirits catch same falling afar.
Awaken Spirits same scent.
Apart, my Spirit I sent.
Where the wind shall blow.
Our same love shall grow.
What we love tomorrow,
We shall not feel today.
Pounding heart beat finger tips,
Listen to them play.

Ruffle A Feather

Ruffle A Feather goes back to Form.
Anger a Country, feel new Reform.
Hands being Fury beats thoughtless Rage.
Anger plotted defeats a battle never a Stage.
Flying faster, watch a Swift.
To plow in swiftly, watch for a snow Drift.
Assault has a bigger blow first Impact.
Leaving few enemies standing now React.
Blood tainted wounds from me stopped, Never.
Taking so many lives, oh Clever.
Fighting other men's Battles.
A Gorilla in a cage so Rattles.
A Warrior smells Death in the Air.
Winter time feel Mother Earth's cold Stare.
Organized surprise Attack.
Leaves enemies on a Back.
Never a man, a Savage.
When all men taken lives away any Age.
From an Indian Chief to Commander in Chief.
History books never changed, what a Belief!

Moon Bear

Once upon time when the moon was sacred there was a Momma Bear who did bare 5 children at once. The smallest was born with white moon on her chest she loved all the animals under the moon; they where her friends, even the butterflies followed her no matter where she went. All the other Bears made fun her for when they did go fishing, not Moon Bear all she wanted do was play in the flowers with the butterflies, she would not eat the fish her friends the Bee and the Butterfly seen this made her heart sad when they seen all the other Bears make fun her.

The Bee and Butterfly said, do not be sad my friend one day they will call upon you then we shall be there for you to help and guide you. All Moon Bear wanted to eat was the berries and sweet honey suckle.

Then one year the ground got so dry when the moon turned on its belly. The fish never came, the creeks and rivers dried away. Then Bears prayed, danced and cried to the moon to send the rains, they still never came the Bears did not know what to do. Then Butterfly seen Moon Bear crying to the moon also for her love was also her family even though they had different ways.

The Butterfly said, we will guide you and your family to the biggest honey suckle vines this made Moon Bear's heart glow with love.

Then Bee said, unto Moon Bear our families are large, we will share our honey with you and your family this harvest moon.

The Butterfly and Bee said go tell your family what we told you. Moon Bear ran back unto the elders telling them what the Butterfly and Bee said. This made the Bears happy, they danced all night under a moon celebrating a harvest moon. From this day on the Bear shared honey with the Bee dancing under the same harvest moon.

This made the Creator glad that all can work together as one, he blessed them the next year by his hand as he turned the moon on its back to send out the rains again. For even the smallest can have the biggest heart for his brothers and sisters. When a Bee first did feed a Bear honey.

From this moon on they shared the land together as one often feeding one another from each other's hand. Wado unto Moon Bear for the biggest heart holding each other close to her heart of love as one the same not indifferent for being different under the same moon.

Look For A Star

Look for a star.
Gone so far.
Tonight is cold.
Hands to fold.
Sun to shine.
Opened bottle wine.
Dream to send.
Mountain wind.
Not alone.
Another day gone.

Samson

My words are few.
My tears are few.
My body is weak.
Just let my spirit speak.
I send my tears as they roll cold.
Treasure them worth more than gold.
Everything happens for reason.
Any day, any season.
Had dream Samson running,
Besides snow white grandfather.
As bow my head thank my father,
Never fence me in again,
As now Samson and I am free let the journey begin.

Scary Owl

Geronimo, leader unto his people,
Medicine man before his first dawn.
One who yawns.
Goyathalay.
Let us pray.
Unto land.
322 brand.
Life we lead.
Heart we bleed.
Cries we cry.
Under same sky.
Children played.
Men prayed.
Temple we wear.
Men that swear.
Two feathered years.
Hundred Apache tears.
Open flood gates.
Patience awaits.
Dreams we save.
Nightmares we gave.
Ending unto.
Morning dew.
Rain crow dues.
Mourning song of love.
White horse white dove.
Name lives forever.
Meet me Gila river.
Let us race .
Never forget thus place.

Wolf never to leave your side.
All day unto all night moon light ride.
Let us race through these dreams.
Land Screech Owl screams.
As old friends.
Unto thus end.
Mending hearts.
Journey starts.
Honor defending.
Hearts mending.
Burning daylight.
Wrong unto right.
Hearts race to a moon.
See you soon.
On Black Cloud.
Hoof beats loud.
Wolf now howls.
Scary owl.

Winter Solitude

Howling winter wind,
Sounds like the earth crying.
Coldness from the hand.
Breathe in frozen breath.
White smoke, smother the ground.
Chill coldness winter fire.
Toes frozen broken glass.
Like barefoot frosty grass.
Tree creak like old bones.
Blowing snow frozen crunchy tracks.
Solitude winter time rest.
Spring knocks on the door.
Sunshine open her window.
Robin love song from his lips.
Eyes open daffodil.
Sky washes his face.
To water, new life.

Sky

Sky, Sky my friend the Sky.
As we catch first wild cloud shut our eyes.
My friend now rides Thunder Cloud.
Joining beside him on my Black Cloud.
Wild Mustangs roll behind us,
As we race through hills.
Our cold breath steams from our nostrils.
Our hearts race with the Clouds.
Our hoof beats thunder across land so loud.
Men look upon us and drop browse.
Through Thunder & Black Cloud plows.
Now your painted black I be white.
When thundering white & black clouds roll into night.
My friend the Sky friends till end so tight.
Only your name shall live forever the unending Sky,
When a Black Cloud cries.

Short Creek

Why was I not born as tree for world to see?
Born me can't you see,
Or a rock to sit on to clear our minds,
Rushing creek to carry burdens away leaving no one behind.
Blooming fresh wild flower no one could resist to pick.
Far away land no one sick.
Wild delicate fern.
Eternal flames in darkness burn.
Desires are many days are few.
Through eyes Grey & I makes one not two.
Man now falls asleep.
While my limbs gently weep.
Our home wild willow.
Mosey rocks our pillow.
Man rushes faster short creek.
Lost another day another week.
Sun now shuts her eye.
Awaken moon alone to numb to cry.
Man knows little about life,
Man knows everything about death.
Forgotten through sands time.
Golden days,
Golden flowers,
Golden rod.
Takes one to heal.
Two to feel.
Before we depart.
No more old Beech trees.
Roasted Beech nut meals.
Carry me far away cold Short creek,

My hands numb no longer I feel.
Carry me gently to land where to heal.
Time before man bottled pills.
Now to shut my eyes.
Darkest blue skies.

White Apache

I rode the seventh white horse,
White Apache rode him proud,
Through the mountains.
Pitter-patter drumming of his feet.
Now he belongs to another man.
Better to have ridden than never ridden at all.
Rode him up the steps to the mansion.
Mansion up on a hill facing south.
Going to sleep watching the sun go to sleep.
Racing shadows on the wind.
Under the moon.
Hope your dreams are as you ride,
Racing taking your breath away.
Down by your favorite swimming hole.
Stuck covered red clay mud.
Easy dancing, feet, feat, feet.
Moon shadows.

Spirits in my Wind

I am the Spirit in
The wind that blows.
From north, south, east,
And west dancing tumble
Weeds as I shall go.
Blowing across deserts
Into tallest hills.
Sending out my northern
Winter time chills.
In springtime feel
My warm kiss.
Kissing cold ground,
Springing forth only,
Gardens we all shall miss.
Feeling my hot breath,
In the summer time.
Listen to my soft voice,
As wind chimes.
Listen to my warning when
My breath blows in a fall.
Dancing with your beauty,
That is in us all.

Turkey Day

Who, Who awakes thus Owl.
Golden sun corral.
Gobble, Gobble not I.
Ha ha, said Crow, unto the Sky.
Fly down Pine tree roost.
Spread wings, gentle wind boost.
Turkey feather, brown as forest.
Strut like opening blossom florist.
Boom, Boom, now thus silence.
Turkey spur violence.
Beautiful turkey tail.
Empty shot gun shell.
Thus be no thanksgiving forget to tell.
My meat no longer worthy to eat.
Turkey bells, turkey feet.
Law of the land, you kill, you eat
Let me repeat, you kill, you eat.
Smelly feet.
Turkey beard prize.
Last supper size.
Broken arrows.
Beyond river narrows.
Another sun we will see.
Bleeding red cedar tree.

Wolf Tracks Wolf Tracks Wolf Tracks

Wolf tracks, Wolf tracks, Wolf tracks.
Muddy creek banks.
Swimming hole, fish tanks.
Wolf path, Wolf den.
Opossum grin.
Wolf pup, Wolf pup.
Suns coming up.
Full moon night.
To hot summer light.
Till frost begins to fly.
Lonesome Wolf cry.
Only winter hide not dawn.
High on ridge shinny Braun.
Wolf tracks, Wolf tracks, Wolf tracks.

Butterfly Dancer

You are thy Butterfly Dancer.
With beauty and grace you fly.
You are thy Butterfly Dancer.
Reaching thy four corners.
With thy tender love.
Flying in thy wind.
Fly graceful Butterfly Dancer.
When thy ever needs to cry.
Thus look for you on thus,
Mountain in thy sky.

Beauty Within

Feel the darkness within the deep wilderness.
Creatures seeking freedom from hunger, be not bewildered.
Hear even beauty from the song
Even deep into the moonlight, echoing into dark caverns.
Dancing, new aroma fresh bloomed lavender.
Smell the fresh bloomed honeysuckle
Tempting into sweet bliss.
Dew falling fast moistening lips as a sweet moist kiss.
Run not as a wild beast.
Searching for the quick feast.
Enjoying the moon glisten across the sparkling river.
Cold chills distant howl spine now quivers.
Call from the wild sometimes a sweet song.
Other times growling, saying you don't belong.
Fear not absorb the beauty deep into the eye.
As looking in the star covered sky.
Touching the beauty with the naked hand, be not amazed.
As sparkling eyes now star gaze.
Shooting star caught from corner eye
Following until it disappears.
Watching deeply wishing to reappear.
Silence broken owls start singing.
Walking closer, ears now ringing.
Frogs, I notice are singing parked on the creek bank.
Some deeper, maybe older, wiser higher rank.
Feel the beauty from ears not eyes beholding.
Little things also treasures golden.
Tis the Season. Enjoy without reason.
They say this most depressing time of year.
Thought throw a curve ball and wish you great cheer.

Dark Raven

Dark Raven watching, listening,
High atop the Mountain.
Her cry, tears rolling like broken fountain.
Raven descending to her pain.
Taking away tears as soft rain.
Washing her bleeding tainted heart.
From new life same as worlds apart.
Silence rendered new song her tender lips singing.
Words tender soft Nightingale's voice ringing.
Across the land silence broken away from bitterness.
Melting many hearts, new sweetness.
Final chapter as her soft touch among my temple.
Take not life from minds made simple.
They being rooted in shallow dirt.
I shall wash away their agony tighten not the girth.
Etching words into thee soul covering all to uttermost.
One memory shall be worth more
Than a thousand words on any coast.
Earth only lent to us from our children hear my tone.
Soul filled hunger gone.
Into her eyes behind locked chains forbidden.
Removing pain that is hidden.
Raven returning with her Demon.
Cast into my pit without reason.
Her memory burnt deep inside from new eyes.
Her Happiness, Joy, Love,
Warming the soft blue northern skies.

Night Owl

Her protection an owl, not only a screech.
Searching her demons, plucking out eyes.
Now a lesson to teach.
Never seeing a beauty molten from gold.
No eyes now screaming in hell, a soul now sold.
Battling her demons alone all these bitter years.
Running the demons in a tomb, many called fears.
For in a world so many cruel ways.
Only haunting her soul never to slay.
Even there riches shall not buy a soul when death lays in a bed.
Speaking not simple words in a world half dead.
Your speaking live for today.
Never speaking words as death shall slay.
Destiny most fear for no one shall live forever.
No degree a fox shall even be so clever.
Speaking not a forked tongue.
To be alive wait not listening, no death bell ever rung.
Never take back bitters years.
Even in a closet hidden fears.
For a purpose we only borrowed,
This life from our children now being old.
Why do you wait for a final chapter to unfold?

Oh Come Sail Away

Oh, Come sail away with me in rough waters.
Make the sweet trip even hotter.
Open waters the open man.
Born to be free & I never ran.
Lets ride the high tide.
Making a one hell ride.
Without the calm waters full sail.
Hesitate, not hold on without being frail.
We can make love while the sunsets.
In my hands, do not fret.
Riding the waves as the sun rises.
Fear not without effort, knowing not until one tries.
As Captain I will let you take full stern.
Still the task you shall learn.
Every boat handles a different way.
Now left to you what do you say.

Seven Seas

Take A Ship By the Stern.
One Can Live And Learn.
Listen to the Devil's Tongue.
Even life without a Lung.
Air is never Cheap.
Even bottled in a jug still costs a Heap.
Brain cells die.
Still I will never Cry.
Even I never felt your Pain.
Putting life with a new Strain.
A life shall never end, come to Pass.
Ginseng gives birth with seeds fall from a Mass.
Skip a rock, rod now Cast.
A ripple grows so Fast.
Days gone by cannot be Stopped.
Being more fruitful a tree so Cropped.
Lose one's Health.
Shall take away all your Wealth.
Taken away even I without shall not Die.
Searching for a rainbow falling from a Sky.
Take my seed let it drink from the seven Seas.
When the Seed falls from the Tree's.

Spirit Within

Let my Darkness my story begin.
As I never touched your soft skin.
Your Spirit, I so felt the warm smile.
Hearts made from Gold shall never go out style.
Even a beggar needs some tender kindness,
Unlike harsh words from the mindless.
Everyone breathing shall have scars from pain.
To re-attain composer or to be slain,
From open wounds bleeding hearts.
Misery begins from the start.
Never look outward to judge others.
Loving one another as a sister or a brother.
Destroy not with harsh words their souls.
Have thee not see the worn shoes, look worn soles.
Humans all being different in nature.
Judging at looks, thinking no morals or great stature.
Burden the pain from the sorrowful eyes.
Lending gentle hands, shoulder to lay on to cry.
One day before one departs we all shall reap what we sow,
Taking heed to words from Bestow.
As we shall maybe never meet.
Live then love shall be our feat.
Letting my words, my spirit reflects from your smile.
From the mirror we touched before my last mile.

Feel My Spirits

Hide not away a story chambers so dark.
Listen, I am no dog, I never bark.
Holding moments, oh, so tight my heart in your vein.
Never feel sorrow from my pain.
Only a spirit falling from a eye to refresh.
Under my cloudy spring rain be oh so fresh.
Shut eyes away from pain, better now touching Spirits.
Take away a badge, not a merit.
Dance with me under naked stars this dark night.
Look up into the west a star my eye so bright.
Looking up an angel, my eyes now twinkle.
Never worry as I reach down for my wrinkle.
Straight up stands your hair.
Down your neck my cool breath, feel the air.
I feel the chills in your spine,
When our souls now entwine.
Distracted now a faint owl with bass.
Dance slowly with me now all over the place.
Looking brothers My tall Tree I shall lead.
As we sway feel souls so freed.
A dance lasting a sweet eternity.
The night we never danced in manmade city.
I loved your touch never said good-bye.
For even a wolf shall never cry
To hear a wolf, now howl.
Under a moon we now shall prowl.

Cold Night

Looking deep into the night skies.
Hands like ice frozen thousand years.
Only life glimmer look falling star.
Light our path, we shall follow.
Shine on our Spirit, as we grow cold.
Shall we hold thus no night no more.
For our memory grew so dim.
Like last light upon thus night.
Breath so cold looking for frozen crystals.
Nor our light, go out this sight.
From our spine twain these limbs.
Shaken like 10,000 mountain crystal flakes.
Dancing in our mist glimmering lakes.

Broken Feathers

Grey Wolf whispers down at Still meadows,
Listen Runs with deer.
Come here Walks with Hawks down by Bright Waters.
Sitting Bear listen to a Blue Bird sing,
Watching over Two bears looking on White fawn.
Coon man plays with a Snow flake,
While Running elk follows a Bright spirit.
Dawn has come then gone since seen two more bears.
Lady bear chases Bear,
Raining horse run away from Two many snakes.
Sun now sets over Corn silk way,
Maybe we will give life over another day.
For we are never free until we die,
Then we will own the sky.
Few are forgot least not the last.
Red and yellow sunset another full moon.
Spring forth flower beds from life going to sleep.
Standing water.
Sweet dreams Silver Fox whispers in the night.
Stumbling bear.

Black Gold

Black gold you do not see.
You will smell across the sea.
No more will I ride my pony up this mountain,
Now flat as can be.
Progression of man with his dirty hands.
I be no better than him,
The number I wear his brand.
Makes me wonder where I stand.
Not on this mountain in the sky.
Alone not I stand hear Mother cry.
Tears dried away,
Mother stomach upset her hands grow old.
Broken bones so cold.
I wear the mark of the hawk.
Let us not talk.
Whispers in the wind.
To the end.

Snow

It is going to snow, don't you know.
From out the shadows comes the snow.
Snow white, darkest night.
Warming blanket covers snow angel bed.
Winter solstice lion before the lamb.
Soon be spring, tonight snow will sing.
For it was written in the snows long ago.
Tracked her little foot prints in the snow.
Now my bed made of snow.
Just waiting for her face to show.
Now I whisper let it snow, before the dance meet me dream.
Cold heart warm fire melts the snow another day long ago.

Snow Angel

Frozen in time, watch it snow.
Last day month blinding snow.
Blinding blizzard 2010.
Snow, snow, snow.
Watch it snow.
Pray you know.
Half past hour.
Snow Angel.
Lion before the lamb.
ooh-nah-jee.

Munity

Immune systems can grow weak.
Then hard to rebuild best try to keep strong.
Life the sweet taste pure honey every day.
In weakness Echinacea and gold seal can help rebuild,
As a virgin from the olive.
Prayers then dreams went as smoke into the night.
The wind weak then grew strong the wolf howl long,
Bow from the pine broke his needles of green.
From the cedar limb green unto the blood,
From center of the vein.
Pure from the land fresh tobacco.
White frost open blooms white leaf stalk life everlasting.
Shhhhh, catnip in the air, lingers wild ginger.

Grandmother Flower

Grandmother Flower fall from the sky.
Where you come, where you be.
Water this seed thirsty we be.
Fertile soil, plant my root.
From the heart blood flowing vein,
Let the sun warm my touch.
Prickly thistle in my Spirit,
Hummingbird softly sings.
Sweet honey, busy bees.
Life breathing vapor,
Mother Sunshine upon my hands.
Humming bees sing to me.
Give me rest holy night.
Warm me morning light.
Awake moon shine upon me.
Grandmother flower delicate hands.
Thirteen moons in a vapor.

Dreams

Dream Catcher

As we get tangled in web we weave.
Our dreams pass through this Summer's eve.
Everything beginning in a center.
Room for dreams our life time now enter.
Listen the night sings your name.
Finding a new beast to tame.
Sea forgetfulness time forgets.
When life time one hides regrets.
In tomb only to be open, not by man.
Guarded by night guardian, protectors wolf clan.
When down spine, chill arises.
Breathe guardian wolf cry out never presence,
Hidden spirit disguise.
Rest now at peace your guardian protects.
When world turns its back rejects.
Your guardian his name, call out.
Find everlasting beauty this midnight dancing round about.
Days are numbered never giving back.
Live our life wait not upon death react.

Dream Prayer

Birds eat from tree, he becomes the tree.
Man eats from the land, he becomes the land.
Man steals from the land, he becomes thistle.
Sun shall rise.
None so wise.
She whom painted northern skies.
To whom he gave life where Eagle flies.
Hawk to walk.
Walk to talk.
Away from dark and gray.
Everyday Spirits pray.
Peace becomes this stream.
Let us now become this dream.

Dream Seeker

Dream Seeker, want you come dream with me.
Dream Seeker, want you come dream with me.
Under the naked stars this night we be.
Sing to the Moon as he lays on his back.
Slow, slowly, he falls to sleep.
Her limbs sleep now with the moon.
Moon light now only star light.
Song from the flute danced solo this night.
Dream Seeker, want you come dream with me.
Shadows cast upon the ground.
Spirit filled night twain bound.
Silence fell before dawn, awaken song bird.
Pour out our Spirit quarter before moon third.
Moon to full to close the door.
Come dance with me just a little more.

120

Dreams Wide Open

Taste life, taste her breast.
Soft Butterfly wings caress.
Dreams awaken sunset.
Dreams turn Spider net.
Capture, go through.
Dream till morning dew.
Waterfall, cleanse our sin.
Spirit Bird carries our song in thus wind.
To Live, To Love.
To Love, To Live.
To Take Life.
To Give Life.
Hide me in thy bosom from thus fiery red dawn.
Deep in her wilderness, Spotted Fawn.
Eyes wide open let me dream.
Her soft babbling stream.

Innocent

Broken. Dreams never broken.
When warm winds whisper your name soft spoken.
Dreams we make blue.
When we open eyes cloud walking flew.
Innocent desires only shadows in dreams.
When night lost to innocent screams.
We all lust, we all desire.
Black & White fires.
Man makes temptation.
Running wild & free stimulations.
Catching in dreams this web we weave.
Before dream only dream life we leave.
What man be immortal.
Falling down kissing the ground, mortal.
One man fantasy, another to lust.
Before ashes to ashes, dust to dust.

Reflections

As we aimlessly travel this journey we walk.
Fighting every inch, never to balk.
Looking back we come thus far.
Never could man promise tomorrow.
Touching me from the very start.
The little we treasured still played a big part.
For my Angel thus I plea:
Never try to understand the world,
Never try to understand me.
Strive on letting your dreams come oh so true.
As your presence got closer as we grew.
Our walk may been cut short.
For one day when we do not report.
When our last breath leaves this body.
In the future be like just a nobody.
So let's Reflect what we have today.
Chase your dreams running as a great relay.
Hesitate, not amiss without delay.

Dreamy Skies

Tonight let your dream race with the wind.
Dancing unto dawn end.
Dream Dreams come true.
Walking Sky so blue.
Moon pours out thus light.
Thus dream guide night.
Power point in life, swim fish.
Across Sky Sea so blue grant thus wish.
Dream, Dream, Dream, Dream come true.

Spirits That Touch

New fire burns in your Spirit.
I looked in your eyes tonight.
New Spirit, a new Moon this night.
Our hurt & our pain,
Only prisoner in house of vain.
Return to innocence starts at nature.
Mother Nature, nature in man which we nurture.
Forgotten meaning life forgotten smile.
Echoes unto hills a country mile.
Soft voice cries so delicate as a touch me not soft petals.
Garden Eden flourishes away from house precious metals.
Two look only to catch a star.
One body, one moon blazing afar.
Our hearts cry, our eyes cry dry tears.
Strength comes from open doors conqueror fear.
We may never meet Jack.
Song from heart from wolf pack.
Up spines men fear the chills.
Numb to meaning life howling shrills.
This day has grown nigh.
A day no more cries.
Two Spirit's same star catch.
When under Harvest Moon being new from days old,
Our dance in life, now look in shadows of the moon.
Men now watch.
Sing with me this night.
In lonesome pines with choir whippoorwills.
We are only scared of darkness,
Living in darkness dead men shoe deals.
Let us sing unto four corners four places.

Then it shall come to pass why they be four races.
Even so they speak we be no race as we race,
Then walk to talk to the wind,
We are one, we be now hybrid man,
Caught free from a routine lost.

When Our Dreams Will Become True

When our Dreams will become true,
Then Love could be so sublime.
Pure Love Without conditions.
Like two Spirits to be one.
Like many Spirits to be one,
With total Understanding.
Behind Distance and Time.
Let us be flying in this Love.
Let us lose our Fears our Pains.
Sharing all, feeling all.
Be your Friend who becomes you.
Be your Friends who becomes you.
When together we open the windows,
When we are weak, when we are strong,
When we are sad, when we have joy,
When we fall on the ground, when we touch the Stars,
Simple Beauty From a True Love.
No wish to possess or to control,
Which leads to jealousy and pain.
This Pure and True Love will lead us to an infinite Peace.
Eternity of Peace and Love.
Like the sun shining in the bluest sky on the bluest sea,
Like the Stars sparkling in infinite universe.
When our Dreams will become True,
Will we prefer to live in a world of Dreams?
Will we prefer a Life of absolute Peace and Love?

Dreams

Let our dream cross thus mountain dreams.
Take us long ago to thus time now same streams.
Racing with the wind.
Dancing unto the end.
White clouds we race.
Another Spirit Sky face.
Dreams we recall.
Harvest Moon for all.
Dreams we never forget.
Awaken thus fallen sunset.

Dreamy Skies

My Lass, My lass, what words flow,
Smoother than wine,
Sweeter than honey.
World apart.
Spiritual part.
Our dreams our friends.
Long walks crooked river bends.
Tonight lend you my shoulder cry on.
My Spirit be gone by dawn.
Sleep with peace.
Wind shall only cease.
To blow again someday.
Gentle hand now play.
Heart beats slow.
Finger walking show.
Fishing creek backs up,
River dreams crooked toe.
As I shut my eyes.
Another dreamy skies.

Flames of Destiny

Destiny.
Would you look into the eyes of destiny?
Or would you run from fates Destiny?
Will you taste the sweet taste of Destiny?
Or are you going to regret not being fed with Destiny?
Would you meet on a date under the Moon with Destiny?
Or are you going to hide behind locked doors of Destiny?
Are you going to try to judge sweet Destiny?
Or would you try to make the most out of Destiny?
Do you dance to the sweet Music in store with Destiny?
Or will you turn off the sweet Music from the date of Destiny?
Would you get drunk on the Spirit of Destiny?
Or are you just going stay thirsty lips parched from Destiny?
Is your heart racing to meet Destiny?
Or is your heart skipping a beat away
From a chance with a Destiny?
Would you ever watch the sunset with Destiny?
Or would you want to watch the sun rise with Destiny?
Do you ever day dream your first kiss of Destiny?
Or off your lips is it a Nightmare away from Destiny?
Would you worship on your knees sweet Destiny?
Or do you throw on the wayward side
The road away from Destiny?
Would you take hold of the hand of Destiny?
Or are you trying to hide from Destiny?
Life is a ritual road map filled with Destinations to Destiny.
Destiny does not control mankind,
Unless mankind tries to hide from Destiny.

Tender Footprints

My fair maiden grace thou cast thou shadows,
Amongst thus rocks unto thou darkness.
Thus veins flows river of sin unto Spirit fantasy,
Amongst thus land dry bones.
Thus hands are callused unto thus soft touch from thus land.
Thus beauty thou cast upon thus rocks,
Gives thou light unto thus darkness.
Cast out thus sorrows in a river of sin,
As thou stars blanket thus cold hands.
Small tender footprints leaving thus warm heart,
As thus sand disappears from amongst thus foundation.
From farthest heavens Moon guides thus Spirit from thus
Angel unto thus night.
Lips opening thus gate to a garden.
Eternity eating forbidden fruit.
Casting out bread crumbs unto thus meek land.
Set thus free return me unto thus kingdom my castle thus
Rocks, follow cross path golden arches,
Thou light high moon amongst thus dawn new dream.

Many Faces

Laugh at me for being different.
When we all be not indifferent.
We all have many faces.
From all breathing races.
We have a face white and pure as snow.
One can find this no matter where we go.
Our faces turning red from our madness.
Our faces blue with sudden sadness.
Our dark faces for we all hold in a temple called darkness.
Qualities we all behold sharp & clear our sharpness.
To judge one another before a book is read.
Is only a book mislead.
Ashes to Ashes, Dust to Dust.
We all are the same under a crust.
Many mere men tried a bought happiness.
Only leaving such sadness.
In a world where peace has lost a meaning.
Only comes within no redeeming.

Wolf Moon Snow

Had a vision.
Wolf Moon night it came this big snow,
This man got lost in this blizzard,
Wind did freeze the hair on the back of his hand,
Holding a knife.
He walked around in circles,
Until he was dizzy then exhausted he fell.
Upon the snow on his knees.
Then he felt cold warm air down his neck,
Then around him came a Gray Wolf.
He started licking his hands until feeling returned
And Spirit did warm his heart.
Then the Wolf started towards the east,
Turning around whispering with his eyes,
Follow my tracks in the snow.
The man got up then started following the tracks in the snow.
They walked all night.
Until the morning Sun saw the Moon to sleep.
Through the Snow Sun bright light flew this bird,
A Red Tail Hawk singing, look in the Snow.
Support the Buffalo, written in the Snow,
Wolf track, Man track.
Standing amongst them a White Buffalo,
Saying Thank you Man with the knife.
In your hand from his steamy breath.
For it takes a boy to become a man,
It takes a man to become a boy.
Follow what wolf heart,
Follow what man, heart of man
We are the same heart beat from love.
Thank you Stumbling Bear for showing me,
Whom I am, natures cry.
Red Tail wings flicker in the morning warming sun,
Red Tail my Tail drips in the blood of man.

We are all the same,
Time to care spent lives.
All I have to say before my Snow tracks
Melt then I waste to much time
Finding my way home. Thank you.

Treasures of Gold

Looking Back Days of Old.
Reminisce treasure as Gold.
Many roads we shall trod.
Many narrow, some broad.
Treading into back alleys.
Some beautiful valleys.
Life shall never be straight.
Treading new adventures before too damn late.
Going back within memories no life u-turns.
Certainly never cashing life in for a return.
Destiny man creates by his own fate.
Treasure the good, the bad, the ugly tend it all as first rate.
Days slipping faster & faster away.
Until our flesh then bones return to clay.
Even the tree withers then dies returning to dust.
Life cycle we know is fact a must.
Springing fourth new seedlings.
As our generations carry on our siblings.
Heed words not with bitter sorrow.
Promises shall spring fourth what tomorrow.
Growing older not waxed old from resentment.
Reading this not a testament.
Making every opportunity count we live today.
Living takes more than simple words I shall say.
Every opportunity grasp with a tight hold.
Bitter bad times stay upright stay bold.
Even the fouls on the earth.
Are destined to death since birth.

Dances in the Rain

Oh Great Spirit,
I call your name,
Take my hand,
To weak now,
To stand today,
Pick me up,
Your gentle hand,
Turn me around,
Let us dance,
Dance life again,
Unto a heart raging,
Rivers flow love,
Through these veins,
Thank you Great Spirit,
For today,
Chances to dance
In the rain.

www.ingramcontent.com/pod-product-compliance
Lightning Source LLC
Chambersburg PA
CBHW020503030426
42337CB00011B/210